BATTLE O_ _____ ____

A History From Beginning to End

Copyright © 2018 by Hourly History.

Table of Contents

Introduction

Generally regarded as the most significant battle to take place in World War II's Pacific Campaign, the Battle of Midway saw the Americans defeat the Japanese Navy just six months after Japan's devastating attack on Pearl Harbor. Japan's aim was to knock the Americans out as a power player in the Pacific so that Japan could pursue its plans for the Greater East Asia Co-Prosperity Sphere. Coming so soon after Pearl Harbor, when the Japanese bombed the unsuspecting base and inflicted tremendous casualties in terms of both human life and vessels, an attack on Midway Island might have seemed as though a Japanese victory were a foregone conclusion.

But somehow, the U.S. Navy rallied after Pearl Harbor. Although the battleships the USS *Arizona* and USS *Oklahoma* could not be salvaged, repair crews set to work immediately to resurrect the other wounded vessels and get them back in service. Admiral Chester Nimitz was appointed command-in-chief of the Pacific Fleet and to him fell the responsibility of restoring morale and getting the Navy ready to take on the enemy. His task was not a simple one; the Americans were outnumbered in terms of vessels, and the Japanese were sending an armada to attack Midway Island.

Winning at Midway is regarded by historians as a turning point in the war. Historians also ponder what might have happened had Midway been lost. Would the United States have been forced to reduce its "Germany

First" battle plan in order to concentrate on the Pacific? In that event, how would the Allied forces in Europe have managed without the massive infusion of troops, supplies, and momentum that the Americans brought to the war which had begun nearly two years earlier for the Europeans? Would Hawaii, and perhaps even the west coast of the United States, have been vulnerable to Japanese invasion if the Americans had failed to hold Midway Island? Would the Japanese have occupied Australia?

All of these questions continue to fascinate historians decades after the battle. Although these questions remain hypothetical, what is certain is the role that the codebreakers played in the victory. Because the Americans had broken the Japanese code, they knew that the Japanese planned an attack on Midway Island and they knew when the attack was likely to occur. Instead of surprising the American fleet, the Japanese found the United States ready for battle. In defeating the Japanese at Midway, the Americans delivered a stunning blow to Japan's cherished intention of ruling the Pacific as the dominant power in the region. The war would continue, and the Japanese would prove fierce enemies, but the Battle of Midway brought an end to their expansionist plans. From that point on, the tide of victory in the Pacific had turned to favor the Americans and their Allies.

Chapter One

Not Ready for War

"Yesterday, December 7, 1941—a date which will live in infamy—the United States of America was suddenly and deliberately attacked by naval and air forces of the Empire of Japan."

—Franklin D. Roosevelt

For the United States Navy, December 7, 1941, was a brutal coming of age. Just as the American nation, previously isolationist in its attitude towards the war in Europe, was stunned by the Japanese attack on Pearl Harbor, the Navy was unprepared for war, particularly the sort of war that awaited the country after the United States entered World War II. Pearl Harbor, and the presence of the United States in the Pacific, was very different in the years before 1941. But in Franklin Roosevelt, the Navy had a powerful ally who had deep roots in that branch of the military.

President Franklin D. Roosevelt, much earlier in his political career, had served as assistant secretary of the Navy after supporting Woodrow Wilson's re-election campaign in 1916, so his interest in naval matters predated his presidency. When the United States entered the First World War, Roosevelt, who was already a proponent of naval preparedness and early intervention, redoubled his efforts to increase the Navy's role in the conflict.

Serving as assistant secretary was no small task; the Navy, one of the largest of the federal agencies, had an annual budget of $150 million and 65,000 naval and civilian employees. The man who would be president proved to have a knack for administration and cutting through bureaucracy to get jobs done. He was a sailing aficionado in his personal life and had been since a child, but with World War I, the stakes were suddenly higher. His work with the Department of the Navy would prove a useful training ground when he became the nation's commander-in-chief.

After the outbreak of World War I, Roosevelt perceived the need for the U.S. to become involved in the war, but this was not a popular stance until 1917, with the interception of the Zimmerman telegram; the American government learned that Germany had offered to return Texas to the Mexican government if Mexico entered the war on Germany's side. Submarine attacks that had killed Americans were also adding to the country's anger at the Germans. When Germany embarked on unlimited submarine warfare against American ships, Congress followed President Wilson's instructions and declared war on April 2, 1917.

As assistant secretary to the Navy, Roosevelt oversaw two projects designed to use naval forces to strengthen American security: the building of small coastal boasts, and mining the entrance of the North Sea to prevent

German submarines from accessing the Atlantic Ocean. When he went to visit the war front in July 1918, he was the highest-ranking American to visit the British since the U.S. entered the war and his presence was welcomed. Neither he nor the British likely realized it at the time, but there would soon come a moment when America and Great Britain would again be allied against Germany in a global conflict.

Elected president in 1932, Roosevelt was a realist and he knew that, although America sought neutrality in World War II, the country's isolationist stance could not last while the long shadow of Nazi Germany cast itself across Europe. In the Pacific, Japanese aggression was also a concern. Japan had gone to war against China in 1937 and was running out of raw materials and oil that it desperately needed. In 1939, Roosevelt, with a strategy of deterring Japanese aggression in the Pacific, transferred the American Fleet to Pearl Harbor. After July 1941, when the West ended trade with Japan, the Japanese Empire was frantically striving to come up with a plan to take control of the East Indies and Southeast Asia so that it would have a ready supply of oil and minerals.

Although the Navy had already conducted mock attacks nearly a decade before and there was evidence that a Japanese raid on Pearl Harbor could have devastating consequences, the hierarchy refused to believe that the base was vulnerable. They did, however, recognize its strategic value and in 1935, had authorized the spending of $15 million to build a new base for its Air Corps station in the Pacific. In 1940, the Americans held their fleet exercises in Hawaii. On February 1, 1941, the U.S. split its naval forces into the Atlantic and Pacific fleets. The Pacific Fleet's permanent home was to be Pearl Harbor.

Despite these measures, Japan was not regarded as an imminent threat to American interests. Although the Navy sent a warning to its fleet commanders that Japan might attack, the War Department refuted this alarm, saying that they did not perceive a change coming in Japanese foreign policy. Therefore, they assured, there was no need for the commanders to alter their current routine. The government did not think that the Japanese had seaborne aircraft that were capable of overtaking the Army's B-24 bombers. Japan, Washington believed, lacked the military resources for a large-scale Pacific offensive. Hawaii, they felt, was safe.

When the attack came, it did so with crushing force. Not only against the Pacific fleet at Pearl Harbor, but also on the other side of the dateline, December 8, as the Japanese invaded Hong Kong, Wake Island, the Philippines, Thailand, and British Malaya. The Japanese were confident that, after the attack on Pearl Harbor, which left more than 2,400 sailors and civilians dead and 1,000 more wounded, they had dealt a death blow to American power and morale in the Pacific. The toll on vessels was deadly; 188 aircraft were destroyed and 159 were damaged out of a total of 402.

For the nation, the attack on Pearl Harbor unified a people who, until December 7, had been intent on staying out of the war. House Minority Leader Joseph Martin expressed the feeling of unity eloquently when he said,

"There is no politics here. There is only one party when it comes to the integrity and honor of this country." The population was galvanized. After December 7, military enlistments soared. In Boston, recruitment officers had lines with hundreds of men waiting to volunteer as recruiting records were shattered by men eager to sign up for the Army, Navy, Marine Corps, and Coast Guard.

But how could the American Navy fight in the Pacific? By the time the Japanese attack on Pearl Harbor ended, the USS *West Virginia, California,* and *Nevada* had sunk in shallow water; the USS *Oklahoma* had capsized, and the USS *Arizona* was destroyed. Three other battleships, three destroyers, three cruisers, and other small vessels were damaged. But the USS *Pennsylvania,* the Navy's flagship, which had been in dry dock on the day of the attack, only sustained superficial damage. The USS *Tennessee* and *Maryland* were sheltered from the attacked because they had been moored inboard of the damaged *West Virginia* and *Oklahoma.*

There was no time to lose. Navy personnel, tenders, and crewmen began recovery work on the vessels, and by February 1942, the USS *Pennsylvania, Maryland,* and *Tennessee* were either back in service or had been transported via steam to the mainland for final repairs. Likewise, the cruisers *Honolulu, Helena,* and *Raleigh*; destroyers *Shaw* and *Helm*; and repair ship *Vestal.* The heavily damaged USS *Nevada* was also refloated at the same time. By July 1942, the USS *California* and *West Virginia* were refloated and able to join the other ships.

The USS *Oklahoma* and *Arizona*, permanent casualties of the Pearl Harbor attack, could not be rescued.

Despite the carnage, most of the battleships and vessels that had been attacked at Pearl Harbor would live to fight the enemy during the remaining years of the war. However, the Japanese left the skies over Hawaii convinced that they had achieved a mighty victory which would support their Pacific conquests to come. Convinced that the American morale was so beaten by the attack that they would not be able to retaliate, the Japanese had plans to completely destroy the Pacific Fleet.

But there was a ray of hope for the American war effort. Three aircraft carriers were not at Pearl Harbor when the attack came on December 7, 1941, because they were delivering troops to Wake Island and Midway Island. Because battleships were no longer the dominant naval force on the ocean, having been supplanted by aircraft carriers, the U.S. Navy was not destroyed. It was, however, badly crippled. The Japanese were counting on that fact as the next battle for the Pacific would get underway.

For angry Americans eager for revenge, retaliation could not come soon enough. For the sake of morale more than any military strategy, the decision was made to bomb Tokyo and other Japanese cities using long-range bombers. Lieutenant Colonel James Doolittle was in charge of the raid; the bombers were launched from an aircraft carrier commanded by Admiral William "Bull" Halsey.

Shocked that the Americans were able to inflict damage on Japan, the Japanese knew that they had to teach the United States a lesson. The Japanese were determined to prevent any more bombing raids. Believing—incorrectly—that the raid came from Midway Island, the Japanese decided to capture the island.

Chapter Two

The Route to Midway Island

"Before we're through with them, the Japanese language will be spoken only in Hell."

—Vice Admiral William "Bull" Halsey

Just six miles in diameter, located more than one thousand miles away from Pearl Harbor, Midway Island gave no indication in its early history that it would one day become synonymous with a major American naval triumph. The island, which had been discovered in 1859 and annexed by the United States in 1867, had a humble role from 1903 to 1940 as a cable station on the underwater telegraph line between Honolulu-Guam and Manila; it was also an airport for Pan American Airways' *China Clipper.*

Before the start of the war in the Pacific, marines stationed on Midway established a base which could service land, sea, and air forces. While civilian contractors built the structures, the marines oversaw the construction of the fortifications. To defend Midway, they had five-inch guns that were made in 1916 and three-inch guns from 1921. The fortifications, dating from 1905, were also under the marine defenses.

However, 1940 predicted a different forecast for the islands of the Pacific as American security and Japanese aggression seemed at risk to collide. A report on the bases in the Pacific perceived that Midway was second only to Pearl Harbor in its strategic importance, so in March 1940, construction of the Midway Naval Air Station began. By August of the following year, the station was in commission. It had a large seaplane hangar with ramps, an artificial harbor, fuel storage tanks, and some buildings. The Midway Atoll's Sand Island was home to a defense battalion of the Fleet Marine Force and hundreds of construction workers who were civilians; Eastern Island had a 5,300-foot airstrip.

On December 7, 1941, at 6:30 in the morning, Midway learned of the attack on Pearl Harbor. Minutes later, a sentry alerted the garrison that a flashing light had been sighted. Less than two hours after that, two Japanese destroyers began to fire on Midway Island. The attack lasted 54 minutes. When the Japanese left the skies, four defenders of the island were dead, ten wounded; a seaplane had been damaged, the Pan American direction finder knocked out, and a Consolidated PBY Catalina flying boat destroyed. The American command communications and power plant buildings were damaged. The hospital was struck. Thanks to the presence of the civilian contractors, the damaged structures were soon undergoing repairs.

But December 7 vaulted the United States into World War II, and with that escalation came the heightening of the Navy's role in the Pacific against the Japanese. In mid-

April 1942, the Navy's codebreaker Commander Joseph Rochefort warned that the Japanese were planning an attack against eastern New Guinea, to be followed by a bigger attack in the Pacific. Admiral Nimitz guessed that the first attack would attempt to capture Port Moresby and the second would be an attack on Midway Island. Nimitz sent Rear Admiral Frank Jack Fletcher, along with a force that included the carriers *Lexington* and *Yorktown*, to the Coral Sea. Vice Admiral William "Bull" Halsey and the carriers *Enterprise* and *Hornet* were also sent to the South Pacific, but Halsey, who had launched a raid on Tokyo, failed to reach the battle in time.

The year 1942 had been good to the Japanese, winning them success at sea and on land. With their success came expanded goals; in order to eliminate the remaining Allied bases between Japan and Australia, they sought to take New Guinea and the Solomon Islands, adding to their acquisition of the Dutch East Indies. By luring the Americans into battle, they planned to finish what they had started at Pearl Harbor and destroy the American fleet and the carriers they had missed on December 7. As Nimitz suspected, the Japanese planned to send one fleet toward New Guinea, where the primary Allied base was located at Port Moresby; another fleet would go toward Tulagi in the Solomon Islands where they planned to set up a seaplane base. The covering force would center on their aircraft carriers *Shokaku, Zuikaku,* and the light carrier *Shoho.*

At the Battle of the Coral Sea, for the first time in history, aircraft carriers were battling each other instead of ships fighting ships. The carrier aircraft were used to conduct reconnaissance in order to locate and pursue their foes. That historic occasion resulted because the Japanese were attempting to land amphibiously in southeast New Guinea at Port Moresby. But because the Allies had already managed to break the Japanese code, they were able to assemble their fleets in the Coral Sea. Although the Allies were outnumbered by the Japanese in regards to ships, the Japanese had divided their vessels into groups that were widely separated.

Admiral Fletcher's attacks were calculated to ruin Japanese plans to use Port Moresby for reconnaissance. But both sides were hampered by the fact that limited visibility in the operations area meant that they were searching for one another in vain. Fletcher decided to send his main force of three cruisers and escorts in order to block what was deemed the likely route of the Japanese invading fleet. There was a risk associated with his plan—the force which would not have aviation coverage would be vulnerable to an attack from the air by the Japanese.

The Japanese sank the destroyer the USS *Sims* and inflicted significant damage on the USS *Neosho*, an oiler. American aircraft sank the *Shoho*. By May 8, the precarious game of hide-and-seek ended, and the two fleets located each other and launched their available aircraft. The Allies sank the *Shokaku*, knocking it out of action. Owing to a rain squall, the *Zuikaku* was not damaged. The *Lexington* was struck by bombs and torpedoes. When its aviation fuel exploded, the crew was unable to put out the fires. In order to avoid capture by the Japanese, the ship was abandoned and scuttled.

With this new style of battle had come the errors of novices. The American carrier *Lexington* was not camouflaged the way that the other carriers were, and the *Lexington* lost 216 crewmen to aerial bombardment from the Japanese. The *Yorktown* was also hit by the Japanese and would need repairs before it could return to service.

Both sides missed targets or found them only after locating their ordnances. The Americans and Australians lost 665 men and 69 aircraft; the Japanese suffered 1000 casualties, killed or wounded, and 92 carrier aircraft lost. Because the Japanese, without air cover, had to turn back, victory went to the Americans; this would have a significant impact in June when the Japanese and Americans met again at Midway.

Halsey and Fletcher were ordered to return to Pearl Harbor. Nimitz knew what the Japanese had in store for their attack on Midway Island. What Nimitz didn't know was that commander-in-chief of Japan's combined fleet, Admiral Isoroku Yamamoto, the mastermind behind the attack on Pearl Harbor, had a complicated plan designed to exploit his superior numbers.

Chapter Three

The Crucial Codebreaker

"It is now generally known that the American victory over potentially overwhelming odds in the Battle of Midway was made possible mainly through cryptanalysis of radio transmissions the Japanese sent in their naval operational code. Information from this source reached Admiral Chester W. Nimitz. Commander-in-Chief, Pacific Fleet (CinCPac), via the Pearl Harbor radio intelligence unit (Station Hypo)."

—E.B. Potter

Not everyone was as eager to join the global war and there were still isolationists determined to keep the Americans from supporting the war. A story that ran in the *Chicago Tribune* in June 1942 left the reader with the impression that the Japanese codes had been broken. The Espionage Act of 1917 was one option for the government to retaliate against the story, but because of the desire to minimize publicity, the charges were dropped. However, an investigation by a grand jury did generate publicity, and fears reverberated that security had been dangerously compromised. This was not a story that the American government wanted people to know about in June of 1942.

The truth was that the Americans had indeed broken the Japanese codes. The Japanese Navy used book ciphers, which meant that the sender would create a message and then use a codebook to replace common phrases or words with groupings of numbers of letters, then transmit the coded message. When it was received, the recipient had to check the codebook to decode the message. The Japanese had been using codebooks since the 1920s and did not believe that anyone, especially Westerners, could break the codes.

Throughout the 1920s, the United States Navy had not made any effort to break the codes of other countries. Even by the time a decoding department was established late in the 1930s, it was staffed by a single person. Joseph J. Rochefort, who would play a central role in the breaking of the Japanese code after Pearl Harbor, was only the second person to join the department, and when his supervisor was reassigned, it was once again staffed by a single person. But the man who would break the Japanese code did not come to his role via the naval academy. That, and his rebellious, nondeferential personality, would hamper Rochefort's career success in the Navy.

Rochefort had dropped out of high school and gained his commission in World War I through an officer's training program. Although his early work was involved in codebreaking, Rochefort knew that this was not the path to advancement and from 1928 to 1941, he stayed away from communications intelligence, instead studying Japanese and serving as a staff officer for senior admirals. By June 1941, Rochefort was at Pearl Harbor. Rochefort's skills as a linguist, along with his ability to connect fragments of the content taken from Japanese messages and link the pieces into an interpretation of Japanese plans, made him the right man in the right place at the right time.

The codebreaking department had expanded in numbers and in success even before the start of the war. They had decoded messages from Tokyo to the Japanese Embassy in December 1941 which had instructed the embassy staff to close the embassy and destroy the code books. There was no way of knowing when the war would begin, but decoding the message alerted the Americans, who now knew that Japan intended to go to war against the United States.

To protect their system, the Japanese regularly changed their codebooks. The chief Japanese naval code, known as JN25, had a codebook with 90,000 words and phrases. The codebreakers at Station HYPO of the U.S. Navy's Signals Intelligence Unit at Pearl Harbor had the reputation of possessing phenomenal memories, but when memory failed, they used IBM punch-card sorting machines to detect messages that used specific code groups. This left them with an enormous card catalog that indicated the inferences and deductions of the groupings in the JN25 codebook.

By early 1942, the U.S. discovered that when an attack was impending, the target was encoded as AF. But where was AF? There was a code group to indicate locations in JN25 and AF was not known. Some intelligence outfits felt that the target was in the Central Pacific, but naval intelligence in Washington disagreed. Station HYPO set to work to confirm the identity of AF.

Making use of the underwater cable connecting Pearl Harbor and Midway Island, Station HYPO sent orders to Midway Island saying that the desalinization plant had broken down. In order to be certain that the Japanese could understand it if they intercepted the message, it was broadcast without encryption. A message that was encoded in JN25 was reported by the Japanese, who had intercepted the message that AF's desalinization plant was down. Station HYPO now had the confirmation they sought: AF was Midway Island.

Throughout the month of May, Rochefort and his staff worked ceaselessly, decrypting, translating, and reviewing as many as 140 messages in a single day. The week before the final orders came from Admiral Nimitz, the decryptions were being processed at a rate of sometimes one thousand a day. They knew where the attack would take place. The next riddle was when the attack would take place. Station HYPO said late May or early June 1942; Washington DC said late June. But Station HYPO, which had decoded JN25's date encryption, had the correct answer. It was enough to convince Chester Nimitz to use the three carriers that remained in the Pacific in an attempt to ambush the predicted Japanese attack on Midway. The U.S. lost one carrier, the Japanese lost four. Suddenly, the Imperial Japanese Navy was no longer invincible. Breaking the code had given the Americans a victory they desperately needed.

Unfortunately, Station HYPO and Washington, D.C.'s OP-20-G spent the rest of the war feuding. The competition affected the career of Rochefort, who never received a promotion above the rank of captain or was honored with an award or decoration during his lifetime for the work he had done at Station HYPO to break the Japanese code. His brilliance did not, his detractors felt, make up for what was perceived as his derogatory comments about his superior officers.

Rochefort had a powerful ally in Admiral Nimitz, who wanted to recommend him for a Distinguished Service Medal for his work in breaking the Japanese codes. But unfortunately, Rochefort also had powerful enemies who remembered his insults and sarcasm. The success of Station HYPO was resented by rivals at OP-20-G, who were embarrassed that they had failed to provide the correct intelligence. When the brother of Rear Admiral Joseph Redman was critical of the Station HYPO's operation, Rochefort was reassigned. Taken from his cryptanalysis, he was sent to San Francisco to command the floating dry dock ABSD-2 and never again served at sea.

However, he was not without supporters who recognized the significance of his contribution to the victory at Midway. Shortly after World War II ended, the campaign to give Rochefort the Distinguished Service Medal began. In the 1980s, the campaign had renewed support as Admiral "Mac" Showers, who was a colleague of Secretary of the Navy John Lehman, pushed for Rochefort to be posthumously recognized for his work.

Ten years after his death in 1976, Rochefort was awarded the Navy Distinguished Service Medal.

Chapter Four

Nimitz, Commander-in-Chief

"The sea—like life itself—is a stern taskmaster. The best way to get along with either is to learn all you can, then do your best and don't worry—especially about things over which you have no control."

—Charles Henry Nimitz

The man who is credited with the victory at the Battle of Midway has been honored in classic naval fashion; the USS *Nimitz*, a supercarrier and one of the largest warships in the world, bears his name. Before the supercarrier USS *Nimitz* came into being, there was Chester Nimitz, the World War II admiral in command of the American triumph that altered the direction of the war in the Pacific.

Born to his widowed mother on February 24, 1885 in the German community of Fredericksburg, Texas, six months after his father's death, the boy was close to his paternal grandfather, Charles Henry Nimitz, who had served in the German Merchant Marine. The child and his mother lived with Charles Henry in his steamboat-shaped hotel, and to the young boy, his grandfather was the most important man in his life. The hotel had a ship's bridge and a pilot house; later, as Charles Henry's business thrived, he added rooms, balconies, a mast, and a marquee shaped like the bow of a ship so that the nautical image would be enhanced.

The military was in the boy's blood; his grandfather, after coming to the United States, served as a Texas Ranger and then, during the Civil War, as a captain in the Confederate Army. Despite growing up in a hotel shaped like a ship, young Nimitz wanted to be a soldier, not a sailor. First, he wanted an education, and there was no money in the family for college.

When no appointments at West Point were available, Nimitz was able to apply to the United States Naval Academy; his congressman offered the spot to the candidate who was most qualified. With no other means of getting an education, Nimitz applied himself so that he would excel at the three-day examination. His efforts were successful, and he was awarded the spot in 1901 at the age of 15 years old, leaving high school to do so. Nimitz's athletic ability at the Naval Academy came naturally to him, as did mathematics. Because President Theodore Roosevelt was expanding the Navy, there was a need for more junior officers, and graduation was accelerated for Nimitz's class. On January 30, 1905, he graduated with distinction, ranking 7th out of a class of 114.

The midshipman quickly discovered that growing up in a steamboat-shaped hotel was insufficient preparation for an assignment to the Far East. Later, Nimitz admitted, "I got frightfully sea-sick and must confess to some chilling of enthusiasm for the sea." When he was 22 years old and an ensign, he took command of an old destroyer, the USS *Decatur*. In 1908, as the destroyer entered Batangas Harbor south of Manila Bay, Nimitz ran the vessel aground on a mud bank. He was subjected to a court-martial for what the Navy described as "culpable inefficiency in the performance of duty." Charged with neglect of duty, Nimitz was relieved of command of the *Decatur* and sent back to the United States. Service on a gunboat was then followed by orders to report for submarine instruction.

In April 1913, Nimitz married Catherine Vance Freeman, and the couple went to Europe in May of that same year. The trip was not a honeymoon; the Navy was interested in learning more about submarines and the way diesel engines performed in them. Because Nimitz, who also spoke German, had earned the reputation of being the Navy's most outstanding diesel engine expert, he was the candidate as the Navy pursued its decision to experiment with using diesel engines to power ships. His study took him to diesel engine plants in Nuremberg, Germany and Ghent, Belgium.

When he returned to the United States, Nimitz was assigned to supervise the construction and installation of two diesel engines aboard the *Maumee*, a tanker. Late in 1916, when the ship was commissioned, Nimitz was named executive officer and engineer.

The *Maumee* was a refueling vessel for the first squadron of Navy destroyers that were heading across the Atlantic to join the war. When the United States entered

World War I, Nimitz was a member of the staff of the Atlantic submarine commander and it was then that he developed a long-lasting respect for the vessel. The first underwater refueling was conducted under his supervision. As the war was drawing to a close, Nimitz, now a lieutenant commander, was assigned as chief of staff to the commander of the Submarine Force for the U.S. Atlantic Fleet. The intention was for the Submarine Force to prepare to operate with the Allies, but the war ended before the American submarines were able to have an effect on naval battles.

Honors and promotions continued to come Nimitz's way, and late in 1918, he was assigned to the office of the Chief of Naval Operations with additional duties on the Board of Submarine Design. When he was sent to Pearl Harbor in 1920, he was put in charge of a submarine base. The base was completed in a year, and Nimitz remained at Pearl Harbor for a time as the base's first commander.

During the 1920s and much of the 1930s, his career continued to prosper as he commanded ships and submarines, served as an aide to commanders, and established the Naval Reserve Officer Training Corps, the Navy's first. War broke out in Europe in 1939, but Nimitz was called back to serve as Chief of the Bureau of Navigation for the Navy, the position he held when the Japanese attacked Pearl Harbor.

Then, out of 28 flag officers who were senior to him, Nimitz was chosen by President Franklin Roosevelt on December 16 to take command of the Pacific Fleet at Pearl

Harbor. Nimitz's response was an understatement: "It is a great responsibility, and I will do my utmost to meet it."

He was made an admiral, taking command in a ceremony on the top deck of a submarine. Although change of command ceremonies usually were held on board a battleship, this was not possible because the Japanese attack had sunk or damaged the Pearl Harbor battleships. In fact, Nimitz held the submarines in high esteem, stating that he looked to the Submarine Force to carry the load "until our great industrial activity could produce the weapons we so sorely needed to carry the war to the enemy."

As Commander-in-Chief of the Pacific Fleet (CinCPac), Nimitz was in charge of two million men and five thousand ships, giving him more military power than all the previous commanders in all the previous American wars combined. Fortunately, although he knew he had short-term work to do, he had a long-term plan which would, without fanfare, take its toll on Japan. Using his Submarine Force, also known as the Dolphin Navy, Nimitz cut off Japan's logistical flexibility, and that would, over the course of the years of war, starve the country into a weakened state.

Nimitz took control of a fleet that was battered, both in terms of loss of ships and morale. But there was little time for the sailors under his command to brood over the tragedy of Pearl Harbor. The Japanese were on the move, and the Americans were determined to stop them. The Battle of Midway would be the test for the new commander and the Pacific Fleet.

Chapter Five

Preparing for Battle

"The whole course of the war in the Pacific may hinge on the developments of the next two or three days."

—CinCPac Command Summary for June 3

Pearl Harbor had been a success for the Japanese, but it was not complete. Admiral Yamamoto developed a plan, Operation Mi, that would lure the U.S. Pacific Fleet out with an attack on Midway Island. The plan was intricate: five different groups of warships had to be coordinated over an expanse of territory that reached from Alaska to the Central Pacific. By attacking the Aleutian Islands off Alaska's western coast, Yamamoto's intention was to distract the Americans away from Midway. The Aleutians also held a strategic interest for Japan; controlling the Aleutians could prevent the United States from launching an attack across the Northern Pacific.

The fleet for the Midway and Aleutian offensives consisted of 200 Japanese warships, transports, and oilers. The armada included eleven battleships; five large fleet aircraft carriers and three light aircraft carriers; twenty-two submarines; twenty-three cruisers; sixty-seven destroyers; and several hundred fighters, torpedo planes, and bombers. The overwhelming force would be what

Japan needed to wipe out the Pacific Fleet and achieve dominance in the region.

The attack was to take place in three stages. On June 4, 1942, Vice Admiral Chuichi Nagumo's First Carrier Striking Force would approach Midway from the northwest in the darkness before dawn. Phase One would involve his four carriers launching aircraft to attack the defenses on Sand and Eastern Islands. After the defenses of Midway were taken out, Vice Admiral Nobutake Kondo would undertake Phase Two. Warships and transports, approaching Midway from the southwest, would land troops to eliminate any remaining resistance and prepare the airfield for Japanese combat aircraft. With Midway neutralized and prepared for occupation by the Japanese, Phase Three had Vice Admiral Nagumo and his carrier force waiting to ambush the United States Pacific Fleet, which the Japanese guessed would arrive sometime around June 6. Their arrival would be their destruction. Waiting in reserve would be Admiral Yamamoto with the battleships of his Main Force west of Midway to come to Nagumo's support if needed.

The amphibious landing on Midway was the plan of Commander Yasumi Toyama, but his planning was impeded by drawbacks. His maps of Midway were out of date. He had no aerial photographs of Midway; the Japanese flying boat that had been assigned to carry out the photographic reconnaissance of Midway had been shot down by a Marine Fighter Squadron back in March. He was unaware of the number of defenders on Midway; the Navy expected 750 Marines, the Army expected 2,000.

Toyama's plan was to simultaneously attack Sand and Eastern Island from the southern side with a landing force of 5,000, led by a pair of elite assault units totaling approximately 3,500 men.

Convinced that Pacific Fleet warships would come from Hawaii to defend Midway once news of the attack was known, the Japanese planned that Admiral Nagumo's First Carrier Striking Force would destroy the fleet. The work that had begun at Pearl Harbor would be concluded at Midway.

The Japanese had enjoyed easy success in their victories thus far, and the swift and deadly attack on Pearl Harbor had made them confident of their abilities. Failing to realize that they had defeated forces who were not expecting attack, rather than coming up against warriors ready to fight, the Japanese had a low opinion of American courage and skill. They assumed that shattered morale would diminish the American fighting spirit. They also expected the Navy to operate in a defensive position as a result of the Japanese previous success.

Their confidence in the element of surprise was why the First Carrier Striking Force was assigned to overwhelm the defenses of Sand and Eastern Island and, that accomplished, to wait off Midway for the arrival of the Pacific Fleet. What they failed to come up with was a plan to handle the unexpected. They didn't know that their code had been broken by the Americans, who, unbeknownst to the Japanese, were preparing for the attack.

After the attack on Pearl Harbor, the troops on Midway Island spent their time training, playing cards and cribbage, and watching the antics of the island's albatrosses, nicknamed "gooney birds." The Navy was recovering from the disaster at Pearl Harbor, salvaging and repairing ships, working swiftly to restore the fleet so that it would be ready to fight. Nimitz, meanwhile, was busy collecting ships to fight the attack. The Japanese had an armada; the Americans only had three aircraft carriers, eight cruisers, fourteen destroyers, and nineteen submarines.

Two carriers, *Enterprise* and *Hornet*, were patrolling the Solomon Islands, having arrived too late to take part in the Battle of the Coral Sea. When a Japanese patrol plane sighted the carriers, the assumption was that the carriers would not be at Midway when the attack got underway. Nimitz ordered the *Enterprise* and *Hornet*, along with the damaged *Yorktown*, to return to Pearl Harbor right away. He needed every ship he could muster, and if he would have more than the Japanese were expecting, so much the better.

Early in May, Admiral Nimitz flew to Midway Island for an inspection and to ask the commanding officers what they needed to defend the island. He promised support for the Japanese attack that, thanks to the codebreakers, he knew was coming: he knew the target, the battle order, and the schedule. Three carriers, reinforced ground defenses, and an air force would be waiting for the Japanese when they arrived.

The marines had been busy digging gun emplacements, putting down sandbags, and putting up shelters. Blasting gelatin, which was used to make booby traps and anti-boat mines, was brought in. Sand and Eastern Islands, just two square miles of land, had 3,000 defenders, along with ground mines, underground shelters, concealed emplacements with guns, and barbed wire to prevent a landing. As they were working, they received word from Nimitz that they had another week to prepare; the Japanese attack expected in late May was instead coming between June 3 and 5. Ships brought guns, tanks, and dive bombers. They also brought 22 pilots, none of whom had ever been in combat.

By the beginning of June, both Sand Island and Eastern Island had defenses encircling them, with anti-aircraft guns and anti-boat guns, 1,500 mines, and booby traps laid along the beaches and under the water. There was an emergency supply of 250 55-gallon gasoline drums. Ammunition dumps were located all over the islands. Food was in place in case it was needed quickly during fighting. Nineteen submarines guarded the approaches to Midway, along with eleven PT boats in the lagoon to provide anti-aircraft support for the ground troops. The Japanese had planned to have submarines in place so that they could be on the lookout for a sortie from Pearl Harbor, but Nimitz had Midway covered.

They were ready with their preparations, but still the defense wasn't coordinated. The radar on Sand Island blipped for albatrosses more than it did for aircraft. There wasn't a coordinated plan for the air operations that would be carried out by Army Air Force, Marine, and Navy pilots and crews. Because of this rough-edged defense plan, the commanders realized that the best strategy for success was probably to attack the carriers with their planes on deck as soon as they were located, a process which required both luck and precision timing. Nimitz realized that the damage to the Japanese carrier flight decks had to be inflicted early in order to prevent recurring attacks. The carrier *Yorktown*, which had been damaged at the Battle of the Coral Sea, had been sent to Pearl Harbor for repairs. Two Japanese carriers had been severely damaged at that same battle, and neither would be able to take part in Midway.

Nimitz summoned Vice Admiral Halsey back from the South Pacific, but as Halsey was ill, Rear Admiral Raymond Spruance relieved him to take the Task Force 16, with its carriers USS *Enterprise* and USS *Hornet*, six cruisers and nine destroyers, the thousand miles to Midway. Spruance, who had no carrier experience and just a week to learn his craft against the genius of Admiral Isoroku Yamamoto, was constantly asking questions. He needed to know how the separate pieces fit into the whole frame of action. Task Force 17, which included two cruisers, five destroyers, and the repaired *Yorktown*, left for Midway on May 30 with Admiral Frank Jack Fletcher in charge.

By June 2, Spruance and Fletcher were 300 miles northeast of Midway. They positioned their vessels to attack the Japanese carrier force on its flank, in order to catch it by surprise when it would come into range.

Chapter Six

The Battle that Changed the Tide of War

"In ticking off the things that weren't done, it was easy to forget the big thing that was done. Against overwhelming odds, with the most meager resources, and often at fearful self-sacrifice, a few determined men reversed the course of the war in the Pacific. Japan would never again take the offensive. Yet the margin was thin—so narrow that almost any man there could say with pride that he personally helped turn the tide at Midway. It was indeed, as General Marshall said in Washington, 'the closest squeak and the greatest victory.'"

—Walter Lord

Dawn on June 3 alerted the CinCPac (Commander-in-Chief Pacific Fleet) staff that radio-intercept stations were picking up traffic indicating that there was unusual activity in the eastern Aleutians. Admiral Nimitz guessed that the flights over Dutch Harbor were Japanese reconnaissance. It appeared to Nimitz that the Japanese attack was progressing according to schedule, but so far, he had only Rochefort's codebreaking to establish Midway as the ultimate target. Several hours went by with no further information. Then, shortly after 11 am, the cable relayed a report that eleven ships were heading westward. When that word came, nine B-17 planes that had been waiting took off, heading west.

Nimitz greeted the news with a huge smile. He had managed to hide his concern, but now, relieved that his defenses were primed for the attack he expected, he sent word to Fletcher. The invasion force had been sighted. The actual striking force was expected the next morning from the northwest. Fog, however, obscured the view all the way to Midway.

By sunset on June 3, Nimitz received word that four Japanese carrier planes had been shot down over the Aleutians. The B-17s that had gone out had attacked the invasion force 570 miles out. Two battleships and two transports were hit, but the CinCPac staff was doubtful that this was correct. Early in the evening, four Catalina amphibious vessels left Midway to hit the invasion force with a torpedo attack. Nimitz's message to his task force commanders assured them that the situation was developing as expected. "Tomorrow," he added, "may be the day you can give them the works."

That night, unaware that the Japanese had canceled their scheduled seaplane reconnaissance, an air-raid warning was sent out to black out the Pearl Harbor Navy Yard. Machine guns were manned. Gun crews went to the stations on the ships in the harbor. Civilian defense workers were summoned to duty in Honolulu. Patients were discharged from Schofield Army Barracks so that there would be room for the expected wounded. It was not a night for sleeping. Nimitz dozed in his office, knowing that he wouldn't be sleeping once the battle got underway. A report during the night from the Catalina amphibians said that two of the invasion force's ships had been torpedoed.

By dawn on June 4, everyone on the CinCPac staff was at their station. Just after 6 am, the message they had been waiting for came. Despite the dense fog, the main body of the Japanese attack was on its way. The First Carrier Striking Force, which had begun the war with the raid on Pearl Harbor six months ago, was en route, and Admiral Nagumo was already launching an air attack on Midway while his ships were hidden behind the overcast skies. He was unaware that American carriers were on his flank.

CinCPac staff assumed that upon receiving the report, all the Midway aircraft had been launched so that none could be caught on the ground. The Midway-based bombers and torpedo planes would be heading out to attack Nagumo's carriers—twenty-eight Marine fighters to stop the oncoming planes. A voice contact from one of Nagumo's search planes had been picked up; American ships had been sighted by the Japanese. But there was no mention of the carriers being sighted. If the ships were part of one of the American carrier groups, the Americans and the Japanese were within attack distance, meaning that the Japanese carrier force was approximately 150 miles away from Midway.

Reports coming in said that American planes had suffered heavy losses, but the dive bombers had hit one carrier, and the B-17s made three hits on two carriers. The message came through that the Japanese had sighted five cruisers, five destroyers, and a carrier. The CinCPac staff wondered what Nagumo would do: would he launch an attack immediately; if so, the Japanese planes returning from Midway would have to stay in the air, at the risk of crashing into the water because they would be low on fuel. Or would Nagumo refuel and rearm the planes before launching, so that his attack would go out with more force? However, if he did this, there would be an hour's delay at the very least. If the Americans, en route, were able to bomb the Japanese carriers while they were refueling and rearming, there would be a massive explosion.

Suddenly, messages stopped arriving to CinCPac. Nimitz demanded to know why, but no one had an answer as to why the information blackout was occurring. When the Japanese sent two long messages from their carrier force, Rochefort's men knew they came from Nagumo's flagship, the *Akagi*. For a time the Japanese search pilot was the only source of information reaching Nimitz about the U.S. carrier forces. CinCPac decided that Nagumo was probably recovering his planes from Midway. Shortly before 9:30 am, Pearl Harbor learned that the invasion force was 320 miles from Midway. Midway aircraft were taking severe losses, but the enemy was apparently not being damaged. Just after 10 am, the *Enterprise* broke silence, "Attack immediately!"

Although the Americans were attempting to learn more from the Japanese, and using every frequency the Japanese had, they couldn't get news. Perhaps, Nimitz and his staff reasoned, the Japanese were not transmitting because they couldn't transmit. They soon learned that the Japanese flagship had been damaged severely, and Nagumo was now with the cruiser.

Fletcher broke radio silence to report that the *Yorktown* had attacked two carriers. Pearl Harbor intercepted a report from a Japanese flight leader: "Attack! Attack! Attack!" Fletcher sent a coded message that his forces had been attacked 150 miles north of Midway. The *Yorktown* had been hit, and Fletcher and staff had transferred to the *Astoria*. The *Yorktown* was hit again, this time about to capsize, and the order was given to abandon ship. But after the crew was rescued and brought out of the water, the *Yorktown* appeared to be no worse off; Fletcher received permission to try to salvage the *Yorktown* while Task Force 16 under Admiral Spruance engaged the enemy.

Spruance sent a dispatch; American plane losses were heavy, and four Japanese carriers were badly damaged. American aircraft were trying to find the source of the planes that were attacking. When the planes that had flown from the *Yorktown* spotted an undamaged carrier, two battleships, three cruisers, and four destroyers, the *Enterprise* and *Hornet* sent forty dive bombers while twelve B-17s left from Midway.

Although the news sounded good by early evening of June 4, Nimitz wasn't celebrating yet. The reports he had received, which indicated that Nagumo's force had been defeated, came from Army aviators who had no specific training in how to assess battle damage at sea. But when

Nimitz received the latest report, he was smiling again. All four Japanese carriers were beyond salvaging. Nimitz message to his forces read: "You who participated in the Battle of Midway today have written a glorious page in our history. I am proud to be associated with you. I estimate that another day of all-out effort on your part will complete the defeat of the enemy."

Yamamoto brought his thwarted attack to an end and ordered a general withdrawal of his forces, but the Americans weren't ready to end the battle. Spruance set off after the Japanese, and on June 6, dive bombers sank one cruiser and left the other so damaged it could barely float.

The Battle of Midway was a clear American victory, but there were losses. The *Yorktown*, on its way back to Pearl Harbor, was torpedoed and sunk by a Japanese submarine. The Japanese landed on two of the Aleutian Islands, Attu and Kiska, without encountering opposition. The victory cost the lives of 307 American men. One carrier and one destroyer sank; 147 aircraft were lost. The Aleutian Islands of Attu and Kiska were lost to the Japanese; Dutch Harbor received moderate damage; Midway installations received extensive damage. For Japan, the goal of finishing off what they had begun at Pearl Harbor ended calamitously; 2,500 men killed; 322 aircraft lost; four carriers sunk; one heavy cruiser sunk, another wrecked; a battleship, an oiler, and three destroyers damaged. For the Japanese, the loss of life took pilots who were experienced and could not easily be replaced.

Admiral Nimitz issued a communiqué on June 6: "Pearl Harbor has now been partially avenged. Vengeance will not be complete until Japanese sea power is reduced to impotence. We have made substantial progress in that direction. Perhaps we will be forgiven if we claim that we are about midway to that objective."

Chapter Seven

The Legacy of the Battle of Midway

"The annals of war at sea present no more intense, heart-shaking shock . . . the qualities of the United States Navy and Air Force and the American race shone forth in splendour."

—Winston Churchill

Historians enjoy playing "what if" with the outcomes of historical events. The Battle of Midway, so conclusively a victory for the Americans, entices the fan of hypothetical history with questions of what might have happened had the Japanese won the battle.

Even with the advantage of military intelligence provided by the codebreakers, it was not a foregone conclusion that Midway would result in an American victory. The battle was fierce. The torpedo squadrons were almost wiped out. The *USS Yorktown* was sunk. Had a squadron commander not seen the wake of a Japanese destroyer that made him suspect the rest of the force was in the vicinity, the dive bombers might have been forced to turn back after their search for the carriers proved unsuccessful.

A Japanese victory at Midway would have left Australia and New Guinea precariously vulnerable. The Japanese would have entered the South Pacific and occupied Fiji, Samoa, Tonga, and the New Hebrides, which would have placed the main supply lines between the United States and Australia in jeopardy. There would have been a threat of invasion and occupation of northern Australia by the Japanese.

Had the Americans lost at Midway, the pressure would have been on the Americans to abandon the emphasis on defeating Germany first because the Pacific would have required immediate attention. If the supply line to Australia was not safe, troop transport and landing vessels would have been needed, necessitating a move from the fighting in Europe to the Pacific. With America forced to concentrate its troops and supplies on the Pacific, the war in Europe would have been extended, perhaps for many months. The Soviet Union might have taken the opportunity, had the United States been occupied with the Japanese, to demonstrate a forceful presence over Western Europe. Over all these events looms the shadow of the atomic bomb; would the United States have dropped a bomb not only on Japan but on Europe as well in order to force the enemy nations to yield to defeat?

Had the codebreakers not been able to break the Japanese code, Midway Island, the only outpost between the Japanese Imperial Navy and Hawaii, would have fallen. Japanese Combined Fleet Commander Admiral Isoroku Yamamoto's plan was to destroy the defenses of Midway, invade the two small island of the atoll, establish a Japanese air base, and position his forces within swift striking distance of Hawaii in order to maximize Japanese control of the Pacific. With Midway done for and Pearl Harbor in line for a final, consuming attack, the west coast of the United States could have been vulnerable.

However, historians are confident that these situations would not have happened. The island of Oahu had more than 100,000 troops on it. Although the Japanese believed that they could capture Hawaii with 45,000 troops, that would have represented an invasion force that was ten times larger than any that they had ever landed amphibiously at a single time.

Another detail which casts doubt on the ability of the Japanese to sustain victory even if they had won at Midway was their domestic situation. Even Admiral Yamamoto, the architect of the attack on Pearl Harbor, did not lose sight of the superior industrial resources of the United States. He was aware that if Japan could not achieve a swift victory, the war would be long and expensive. While the American war machine was revving up production, Japan's economy was showing signs of the strain. Midway was not the death knell for the Empire of Japan, but Japan's losses were higher than American losses. Most of the American aircrews that were brought down were rescued, but the opposite was true for the Japanese that fell to attack. Most of them drowned. The Japanese could not replace the skill and experience of these lost men, which amounted to almost one-third of the Japanese Navy's available aircrews.

After losing at Midway, the Japanese were on the defensive, fighting to hold onto the territory that they had acquired. The Americans were on the offensive. On the home front, Americans rejoiced at the news that Pearl Harbor had been avenged. The war had years to go before the Allies could claim victory, but with the victory at Midway, the United States had served notice that it would be a power to reckon with.

Territory was not the only victory enjoyed by the Americans at the Battle of Midway. One of the lasting legacies of the Battle of Midway is the demonstration of the importance of information in the military. The American codebreakers, which were the forerunners of what is today the Information Dominance Corps, had a direct effect on Admiral Nimitz's battle plans. As U.S. Army Chief of Staff General George C. Marshall explained at the time, "as a result of cryptanalysis we were able to concentrate our limited forces to meet their naval advance on Midway when we otherwise would have been 3,000 miles out of place."

In 2009, the Navy established the Information Dominance Corps, combining representatives from the intelligence, information professional, information warfare, meteorology, space, and oceanography communities under the deputy chief of Naval Operations for Information Dominance. By combining intelligence sources into one unified corps, the Navy is better able to make informed, timely decisions regarding the strategy of the wars it fights.

Addressing the fleet upon this event, Chief of Naval Operations Admiral Jonathan Greenert said, "Though a lifetime has passed since the Battle of Midway, and the world and our Navy have changed in many ways, the lessons of June 1942 still resonate today. The Navy-Marine Corps team, acting decisively in defense of our nation's interests, can project more power, across greater distances, more effectively, than any naval force the world has ever seen. That was demonstrated at Midway and throughout the Pacific in World War II, and maintaining that capability is our charge today."

Made in the USA
Las Vegas, NV
08 February 2024

85446216R00026